BrainSnack®

DRAW with NUMBERS

Andrews McMeel
Publishing®

Kansas City • Sydney • London

Go Fun! BrainSnack® Draw with Numbers

copyright © 2015 by Andrews McMeel Publishing, LLC.
All rights reserved. BrainSnack® Draw with Numbers art
and text by Frank Coussement and Peter De Schepper
copyright © 2015 by PeterFrank tv. All rights reserved.
Printed in the United States of America. No part of
this book may be used or reproduced in any manner
whatsoever without written permission except in the case
of reprints in the context of reviews.

Andrews McMeel Publishing, LLC
an Andrews McMeel Universal company
1130 Walnut Street, Kansas City, Missouri 64106

www.andrewsmcmeel.com

15 16 17 18 19 PAH 10 9 8 7 6 5 4 3 2 1

ISBN: 978-1-4494-7242-9

Made by:
The P. A. Hutchison Company
Address and location of production:
400 Penn Avenue, Mayfield, PA 18433 USA
1st printing – September 21, 2015

ATTENTION: SCHOOLS AND BUSINESSES
Andrews McMeel books are available at quantity
discounts with bulk purchase for educational, business, or
sales promotional use. For information, please e-mail the
Andrews McMeel Publishing Special Sales Department:
specialsales@amuniversal.com.

How To
Draw with Numbers

Above each image you will find the figure(s) you have to use for each step. When necessary, we show a few helplines, which will assist you to draw the figures in their correct proportions.

5	0	3	Finish!

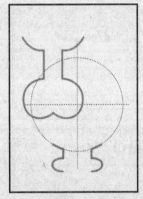 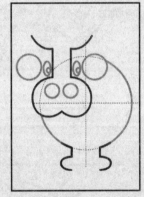  

Step 1
Draw four **5**'s. Use the helplines to place them correctly.

Step 2
Use several **0**'s to make the eyes, ears, and nose. Use the helpline of the big **0** to draw the rest of the body.

Step 3
Use some **3**'s for the hair, the ears, and the end of the tail.

Step 4
Now draw the lines to complete the horns, head, tail, and legs. Finish off the cow with a few spots on the body and a simple tongue.

0 6

8 0

3

Finish!

DRAW WITH NUMBERS

DRAW WITH NUMBERS

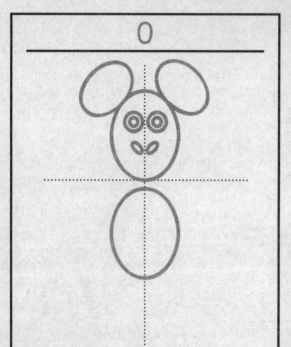

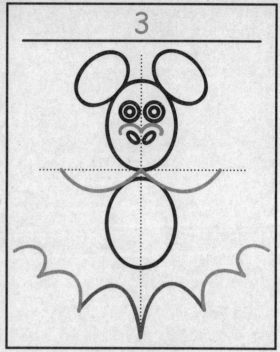

DRAW WITH NUMBERS

2

0

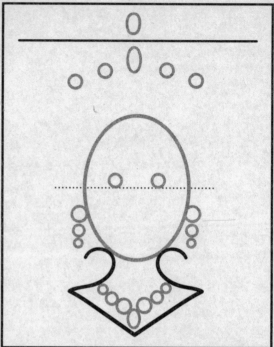

3

Finish!

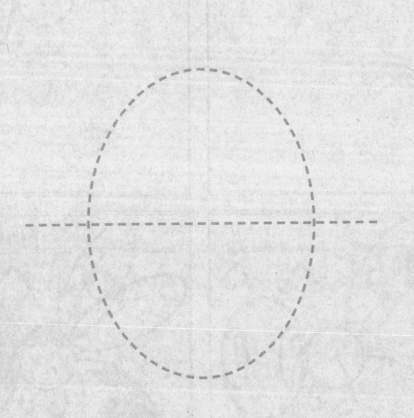

0

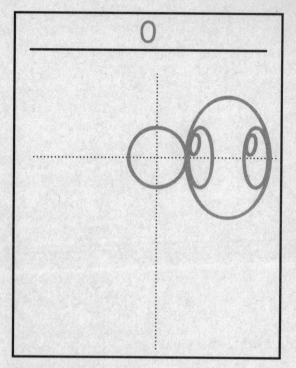

6 7

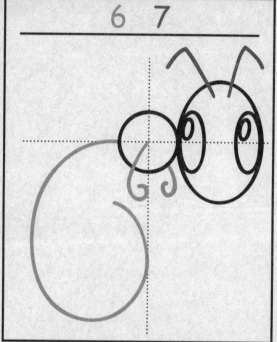

0

Finish!

DRAW WITH NUMBERS

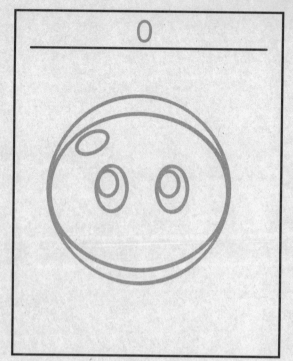

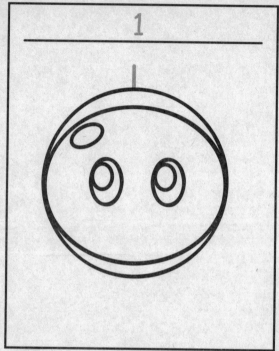

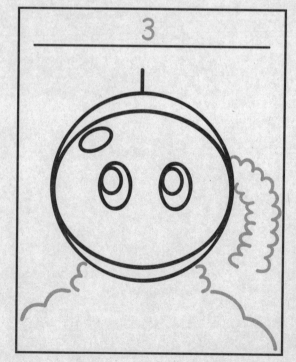

DRAW WITH NUMBERS

0	3
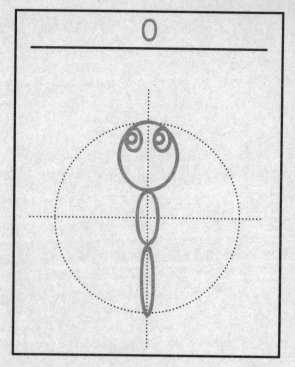	

0	Finish!

DRAW WITH NUMBERS

DRAW WITH NUMBERS

4

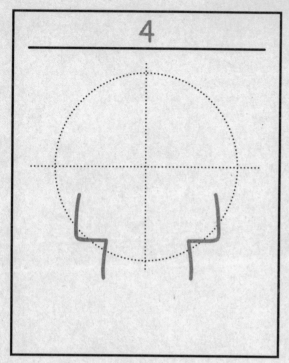

3

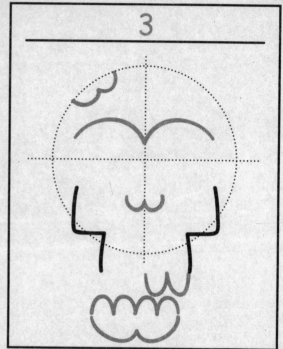

0

Finish!

DRAW WITH NUMBERS

DRAW WITH NUMBERS

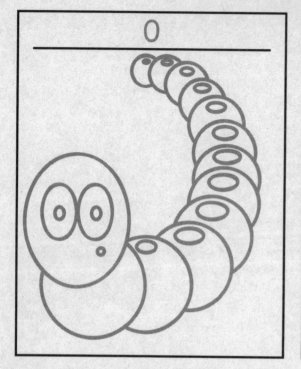

Finish!

DRAW WITH NUMBERS

DRAW WITH NUMBERS

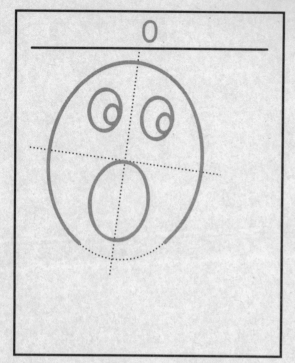

DRAW WITH NUMBERS

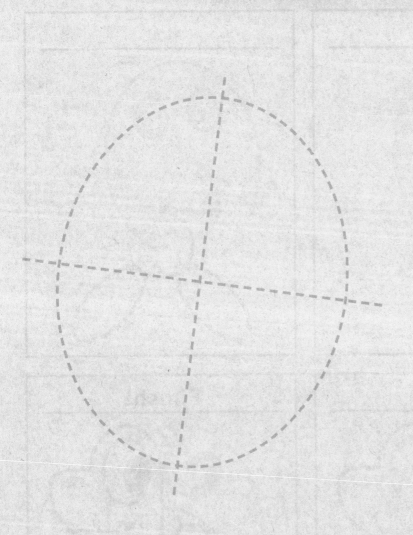

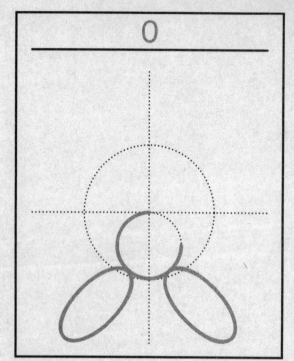

0

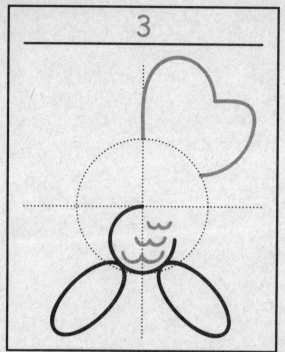

3

0

Finish!

DRAW WITH NUMBERS

DRAW WITH NUMBERS

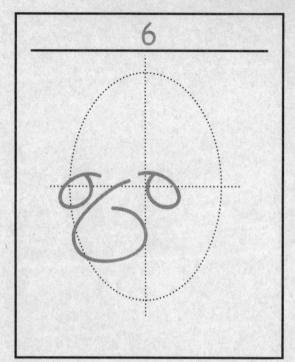

6

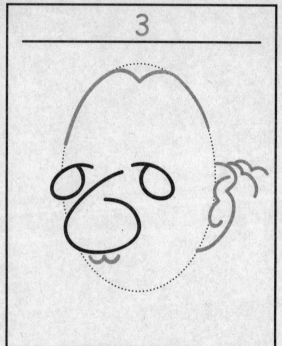

3

8

Finish!

DRAW WITH NUMBERS

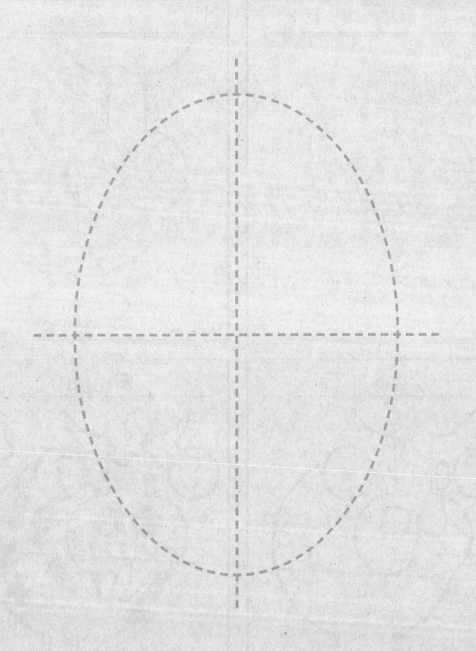

DRAW WITH NUMBERS

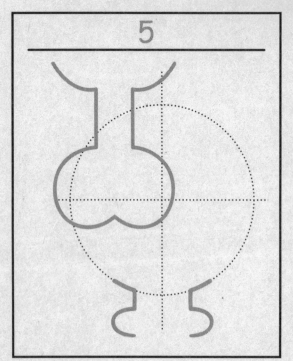

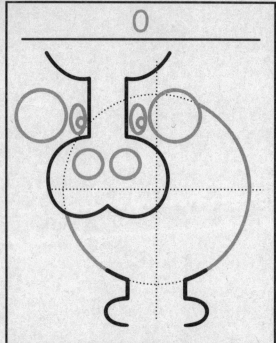

DRAW WITH NUMBERS

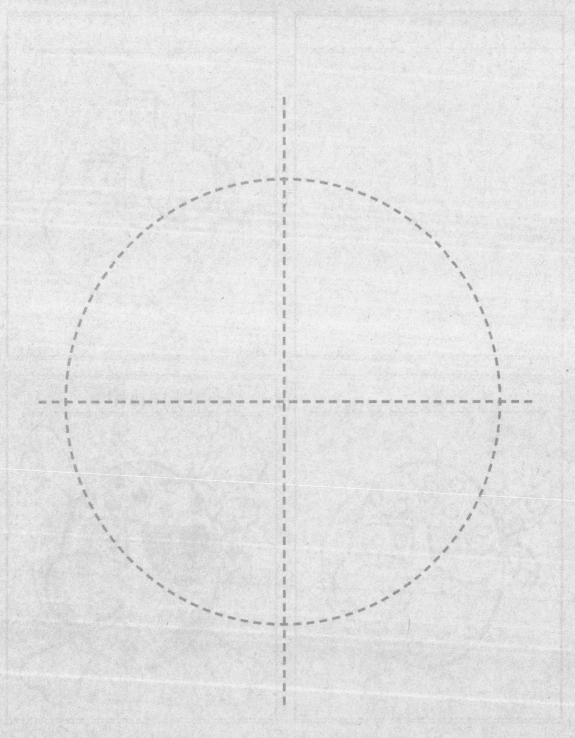

5

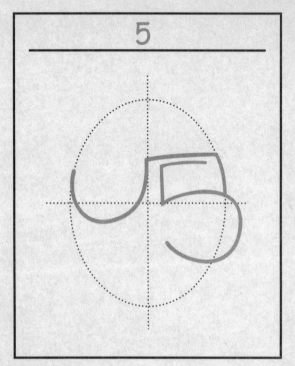

0 8

3

Finish!

DRAW WITH NUMBERS

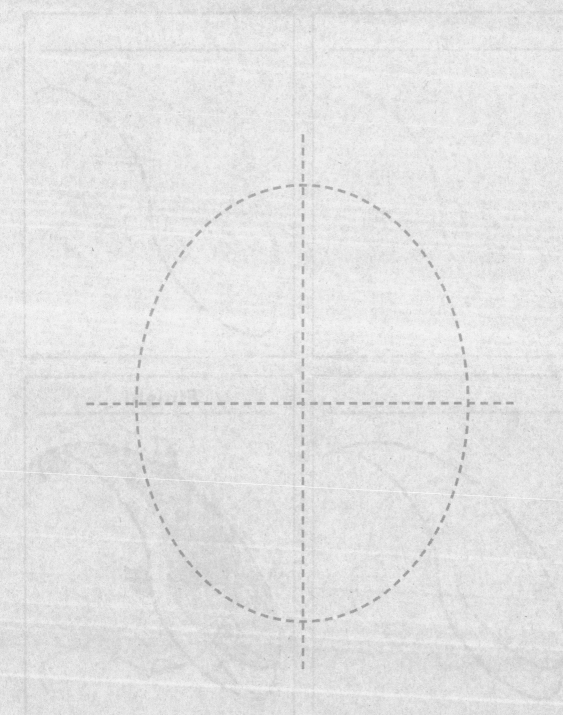

DRAW WITH NUMBERS

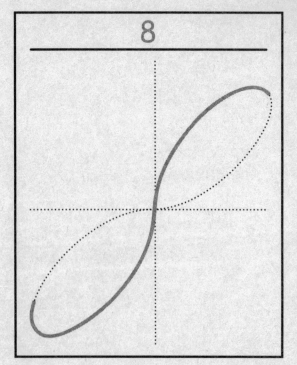

8

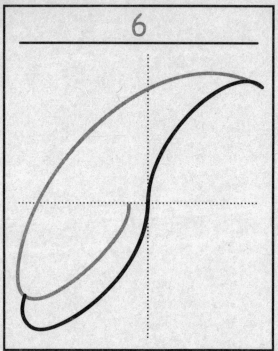

6

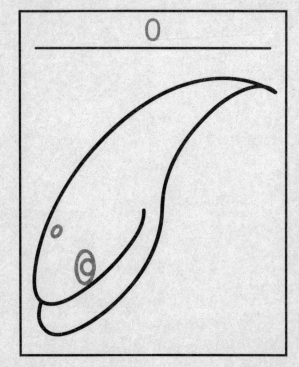

0

Finish!

DRAW WITH NUMBERS

DRAW WITH NUMBERS

6 0

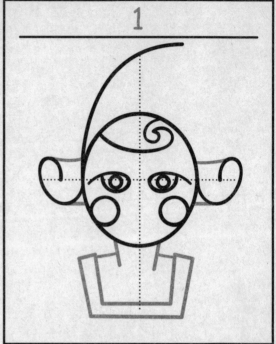

1

3

Finish!

DRAW WITH NUMBERS

DRAW WITH NUMBERS

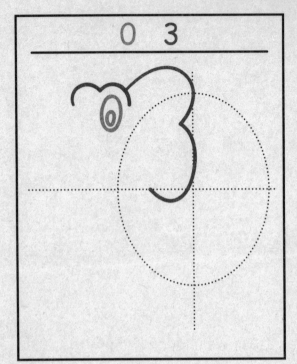

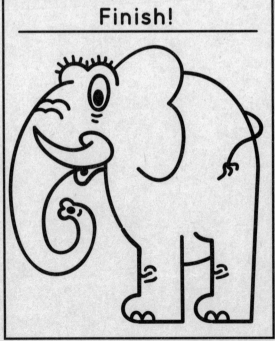

DRAW WITH NUMBERS

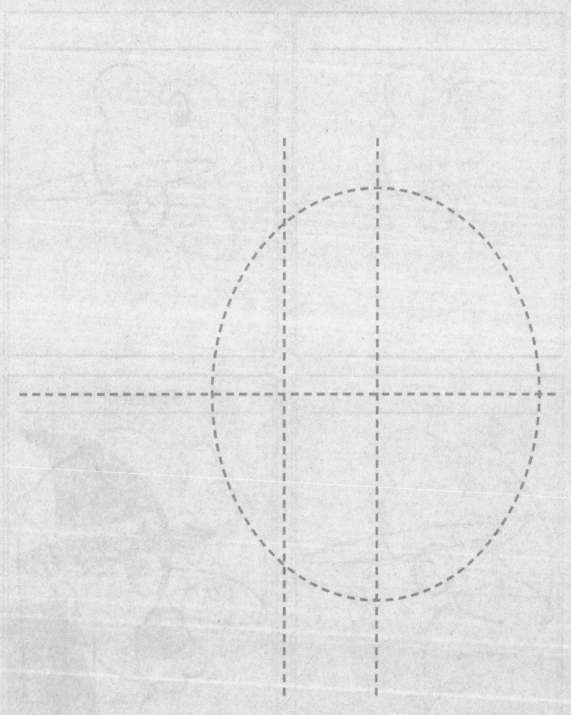

DRAW WITH NUMBERS

0

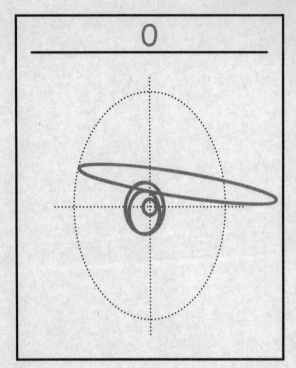

6

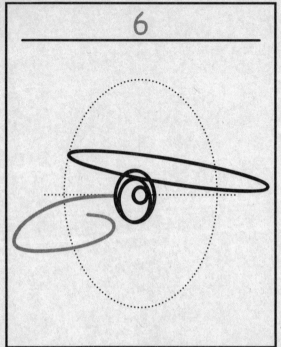

3

Finish!

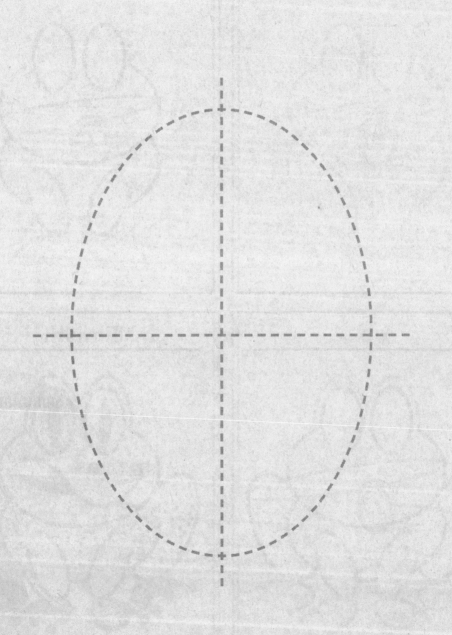

DRAW WITH NUMBERS

0

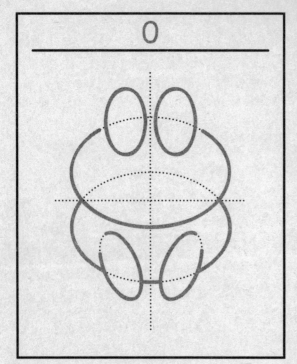

0

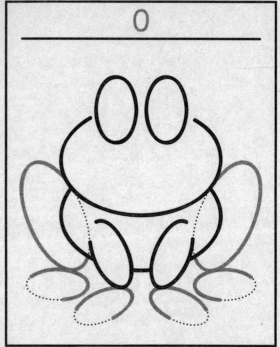

3

Finish!

DRAW WITH NUMBERS

DRAW WITH NUMBERS

5

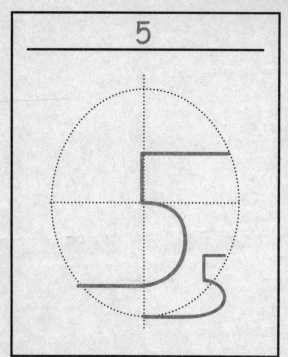

6

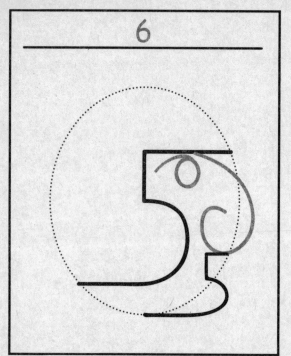

0

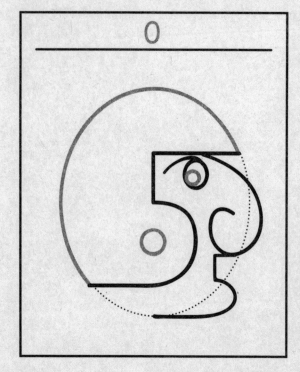

Finish!

DRAW WITH NUMBERS

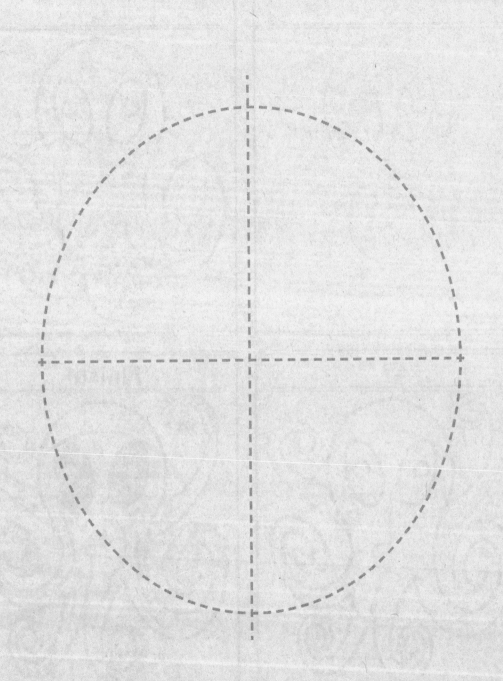

DRAW WITH NUMBERS

0

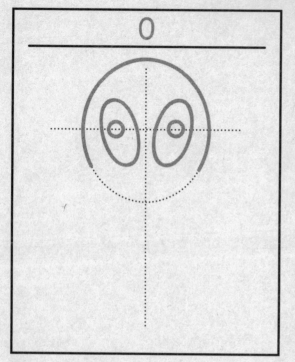

6

9

Finish!

DRAW WITH NUMBERS

DRAW WITH NUMBERS

3 4

0

8

Finish!

DRAW WITH NUMBERS

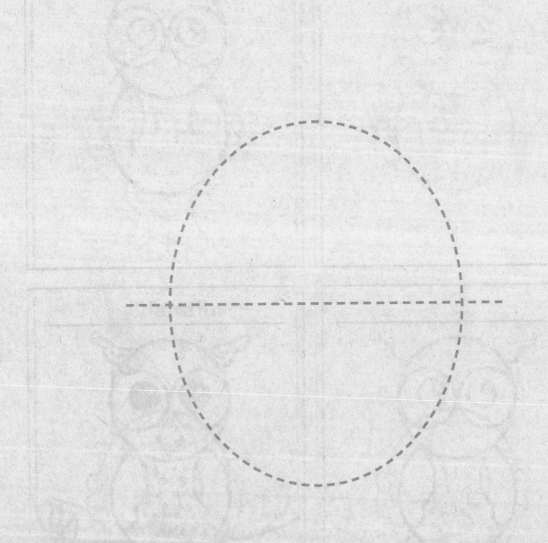

DRAW WITH NUMBERS

0

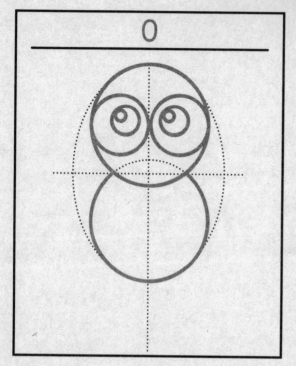

3

0

Finish!

0 6

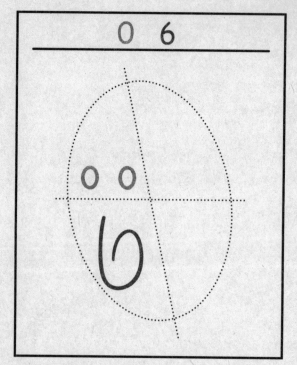

3

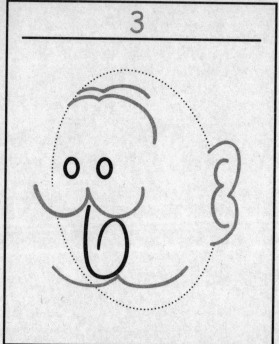

1

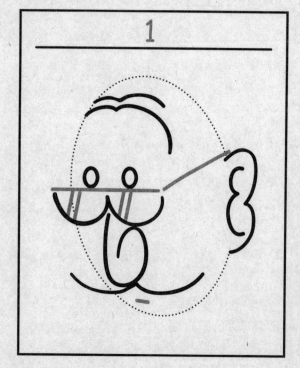

Finish!

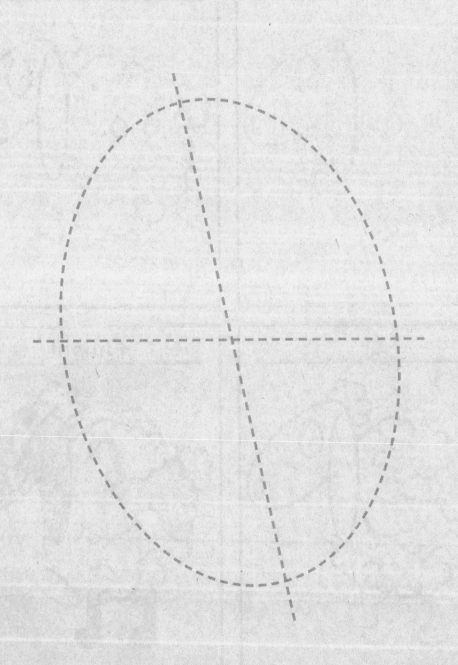

DRAW WITH NUMBERS

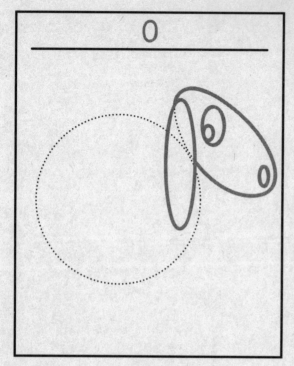

0

3

5

Finish!

DRAW WITH NUMBERS

DRAW WITH NUMBERS

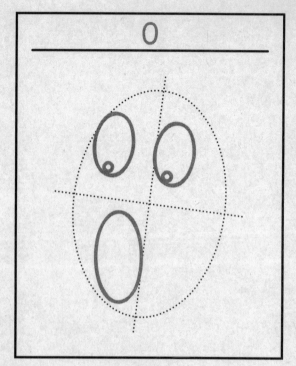

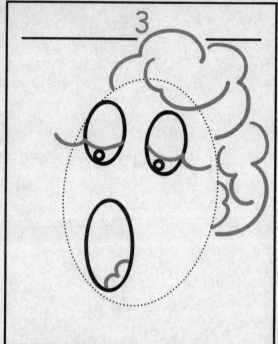

Finish!

DRAW WITH NUMBERS

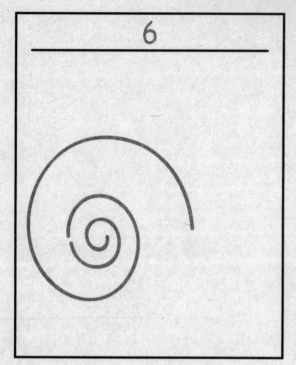

6

3

0

Finish!

DRAW WITH NUMBERS

DRAW WITH NUMBERS

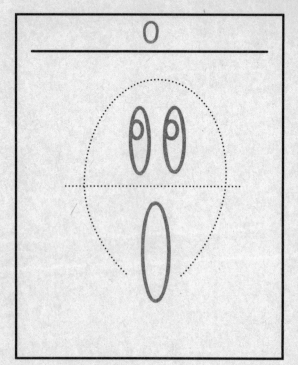

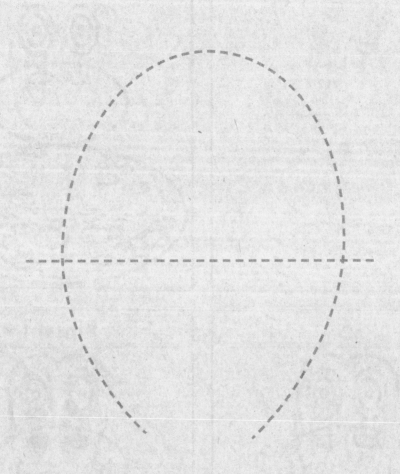

DRAW WITH NUMBERS

0

3

6

Finish!

DRAW WITH NUMBERS

DRAW WITH NUMBERS

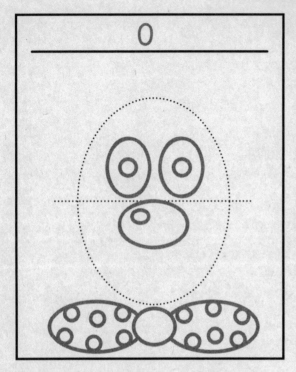

0

3

6

Finish!

DRAW WITH NUMBERS

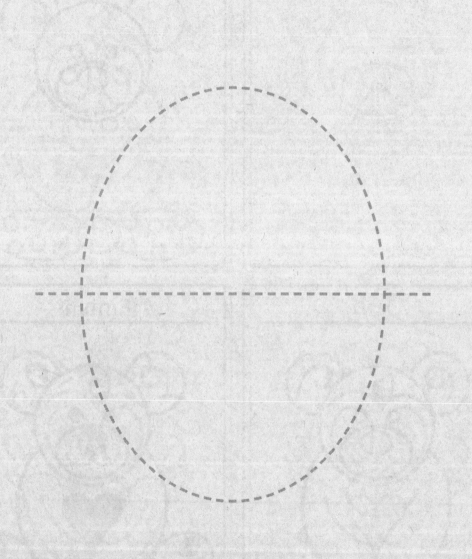

DRAW WITH NUMBERS

0

6

0 3

Finish!

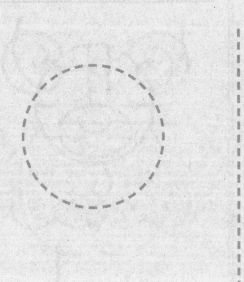

DRAW WITH NUMBERS

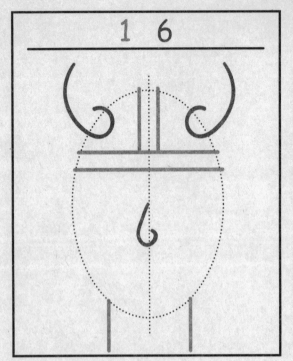

1 6

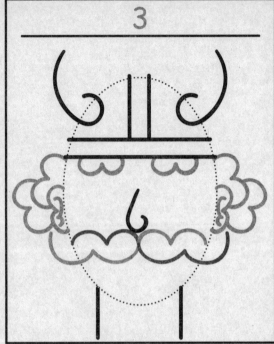

3

0

Finish!

DRAW WITH NUMBERS

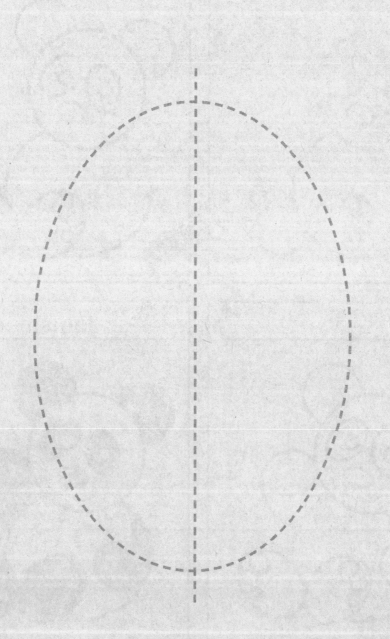

0

6

3

Finish!

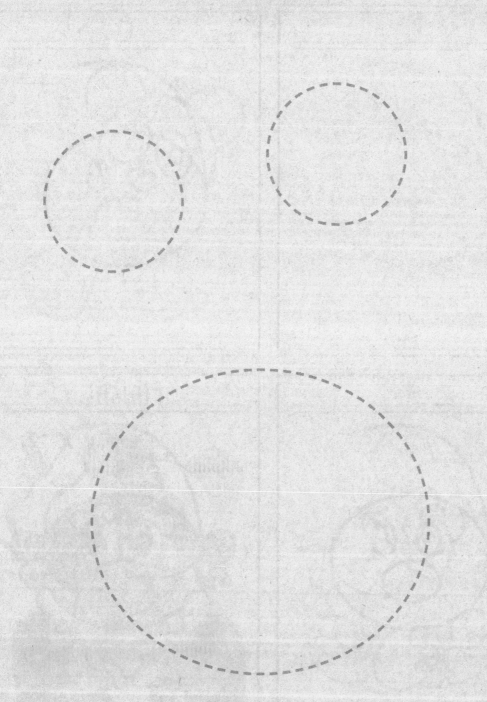

DRAW WITH NUMBERS

6

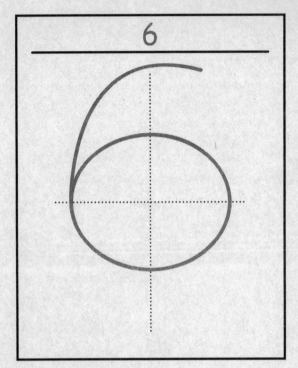

0

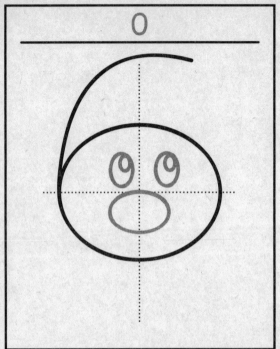

3

Finish!

DRAW WITH NUMBERS

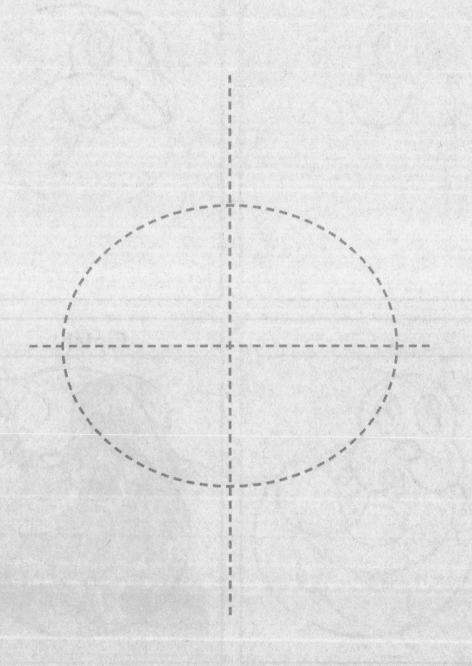

DRAW WITH NUMBERS

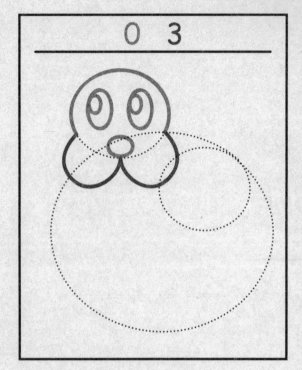

0 3

0

3

Finish!

DRAW WITH NUMBERS

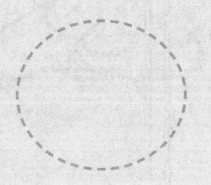

DRAW WITH NUMBERS

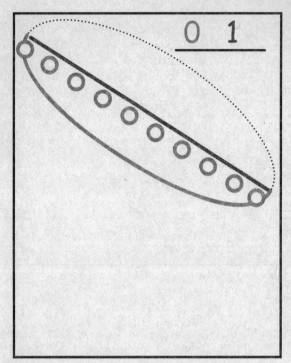

0 1

5 6 1

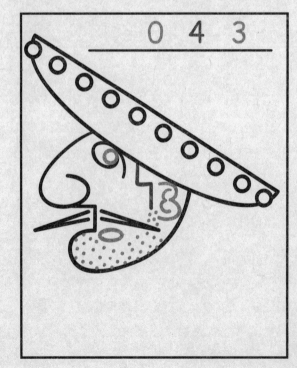

0 4 3

Finish!

DRAW WITH NUMBERS

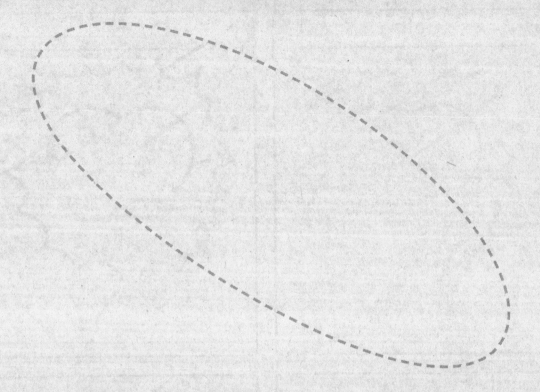

DRAW WITH NUMBERS

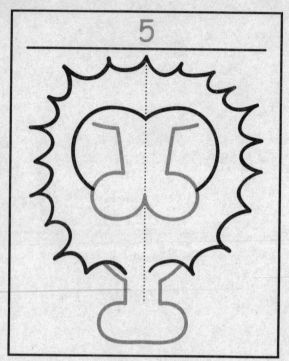

DRAW WITH NUMBERS

DRAW WITH NUMBERS

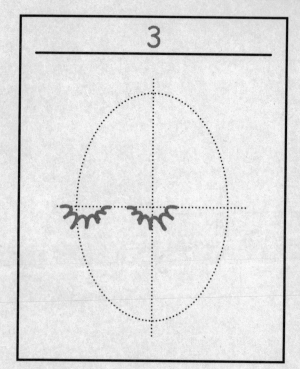

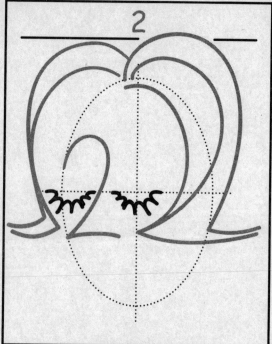

DRAW WITH NUMBERS

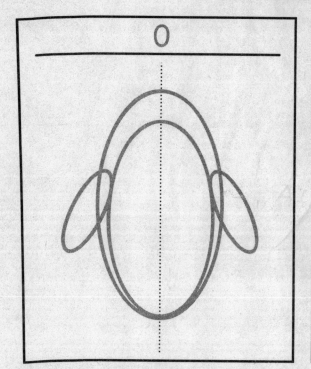

0

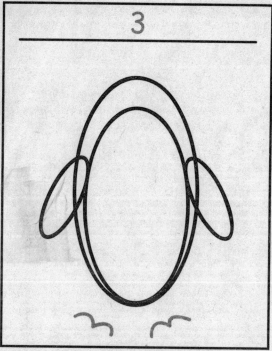

3

6 0

Finish!

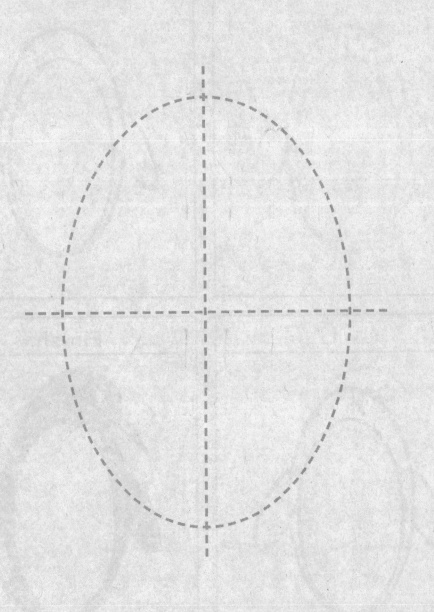

DRAW WITH NUMBERS

DRAW WITH NUMBERS

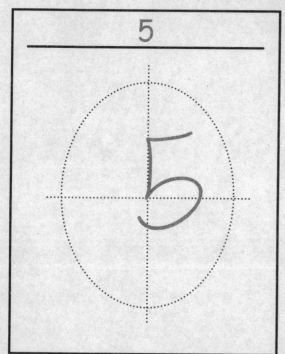

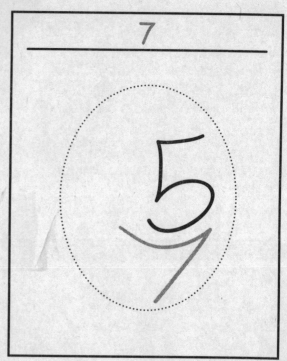

DRAW WITH NUMBERS

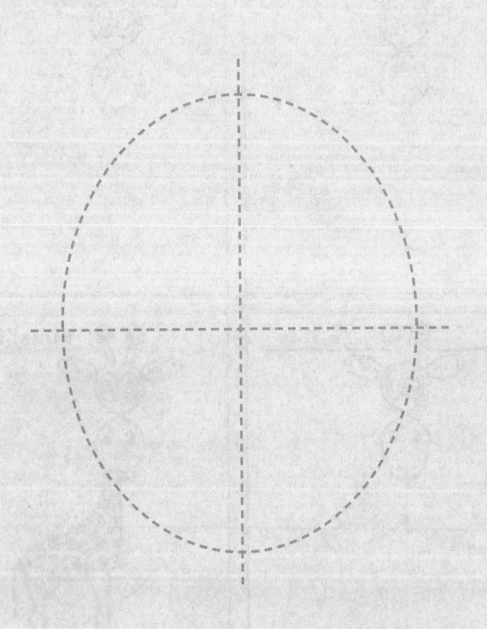

DRAW WITH NUMBERS

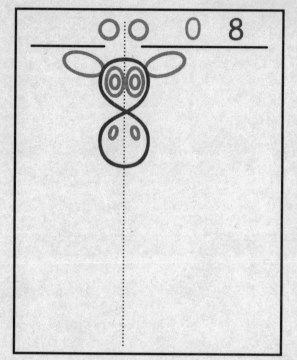

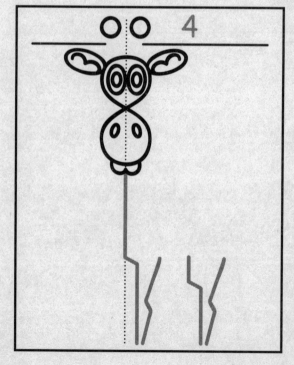

Finish!

DRAW WITH NUMBERS

DRAW WITH NUMBERS

3 4

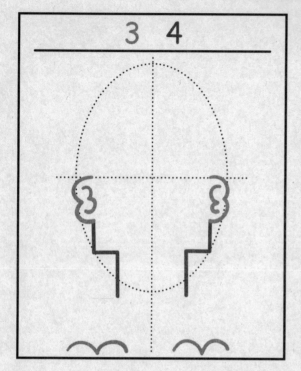

1 5

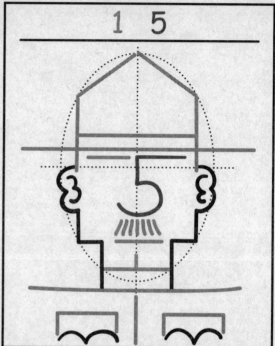

0

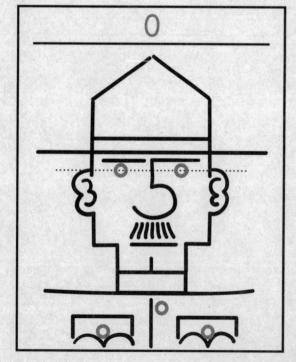

Finish!

DRAW WITH NUMBERS

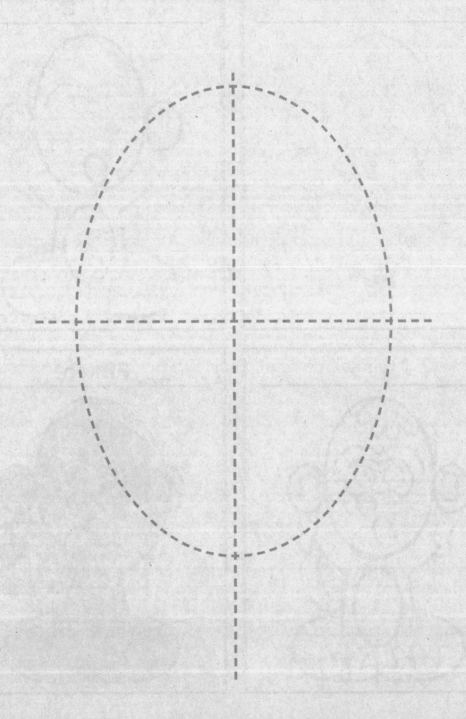

DRAW WITH NUMBERS

0

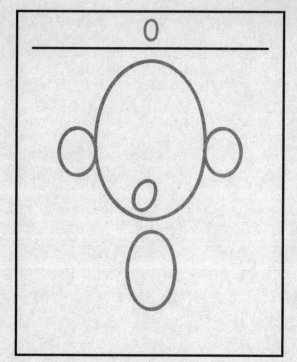

3 5

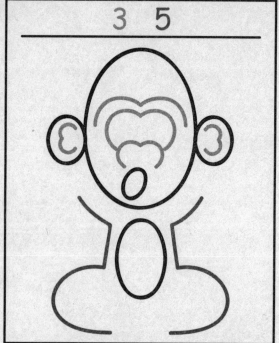

0 3

Finish!

DRAW WITH NUMBERS

DRAW WITH NUMBERS

0

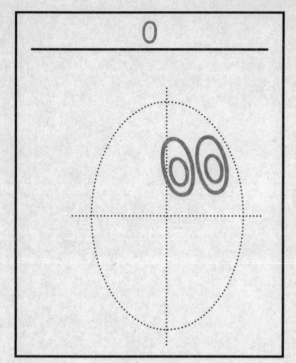

3

0

Finish!

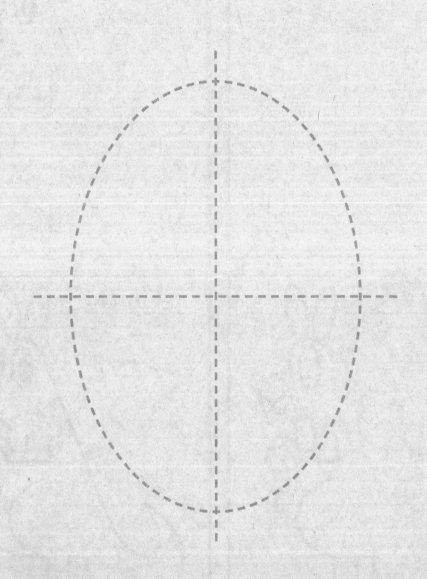

DRAW WITH NUMBERS

DRAW WITH NUMBERS

0

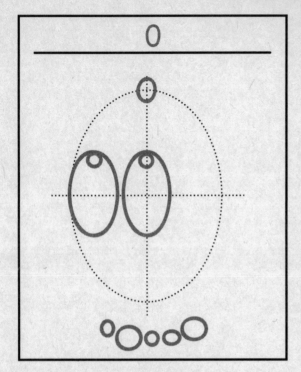

6

3

Finish!

DRAW WITH NUMBERS

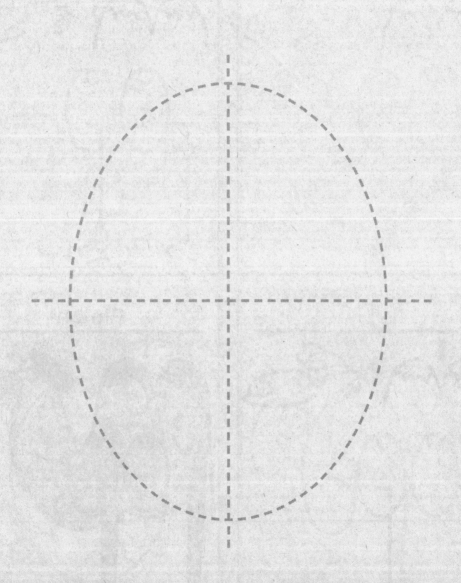

DRAW WITH NUMBERS

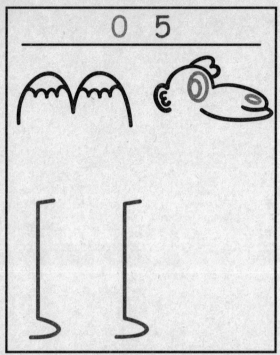

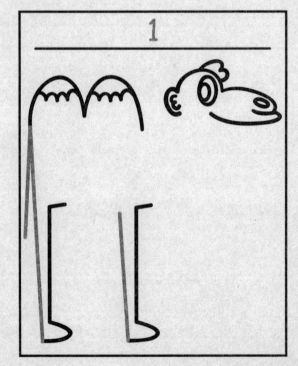

DRAW WITH NUMBERS

DRAW WITH NUMBERS

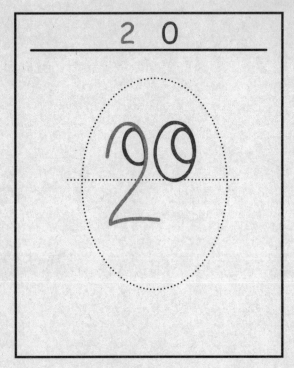

2 0

3

6

Finish!

DRAW WITH NUMBERS

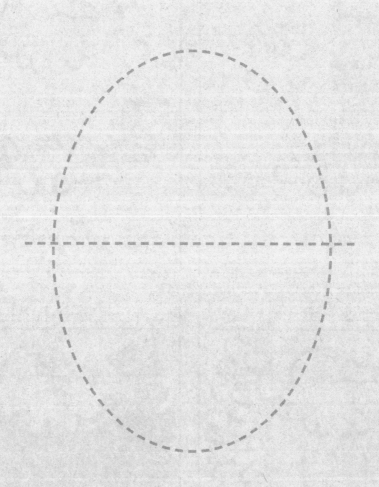

3

3

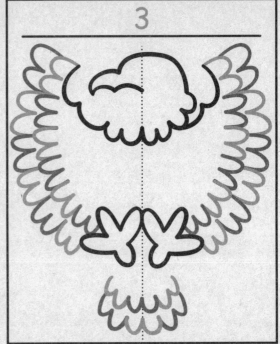

0 1

Finish!

DRAW WITH NUMBERS

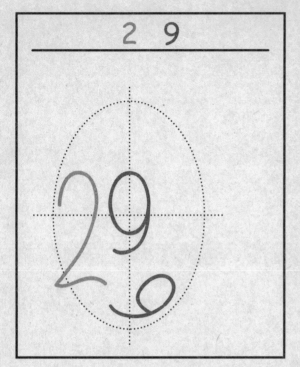

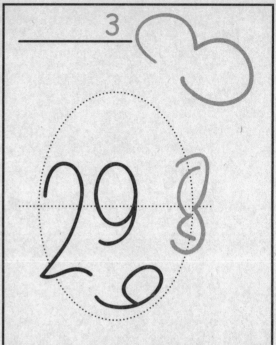

DRAW WITH NUMBERS

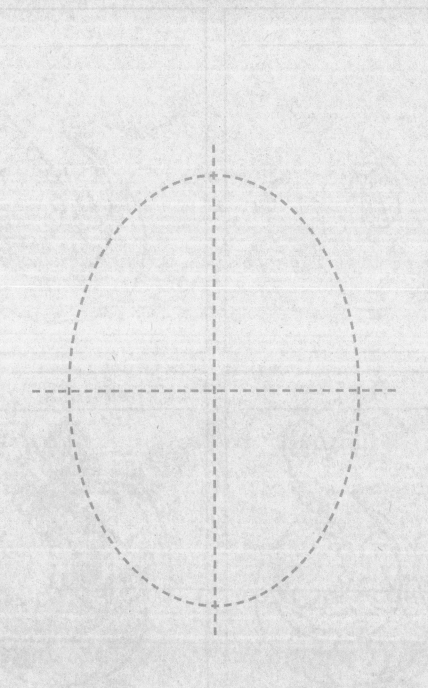

DRAW WITH NUMBERS

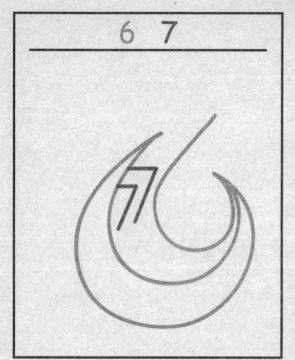

DRAW WITH NUMBERS

DRAW WITH NUMBERS

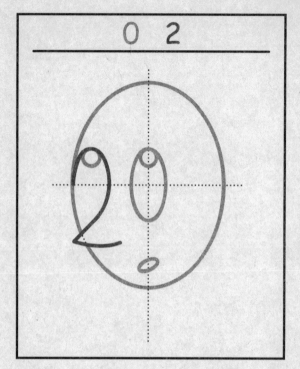

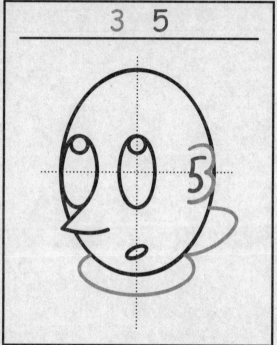

Finish!

DRAW WITH NUMBERS

DRAW WITH NUMBERS

3

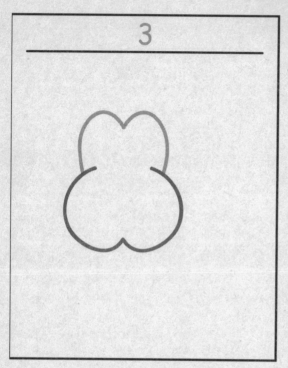

0

3 6

Finish!

DRAW WITH NUMBERS

DRAW WITH NUMBERS

0

3

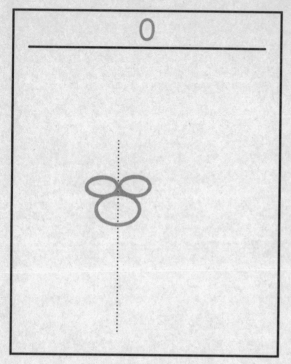

3   6

Finish!

DRAW WITH NUMBERS

DRAW WITH NUMBERS

DRAW WITH NUMBERS

DRAW WITH NUMBERS

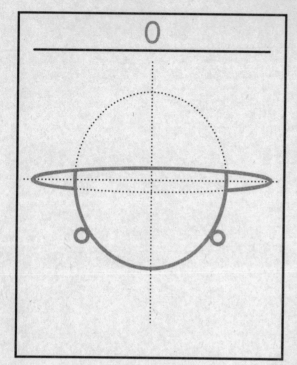

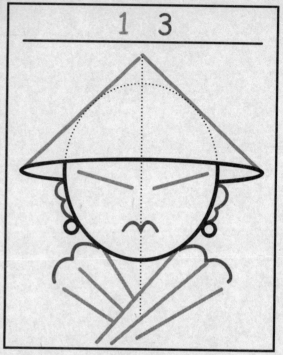

DRAW WITH NUMBERS

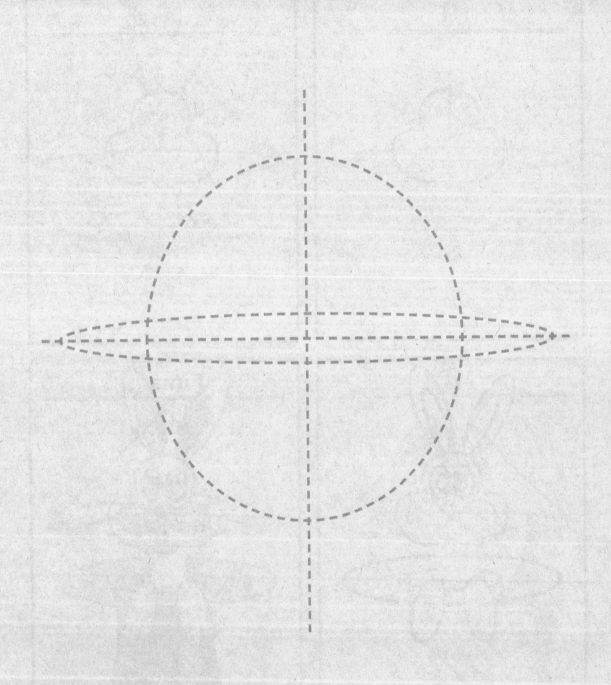

DRAW WITH NUMBERS

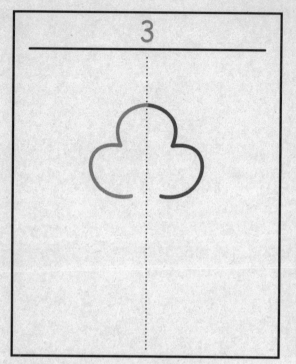

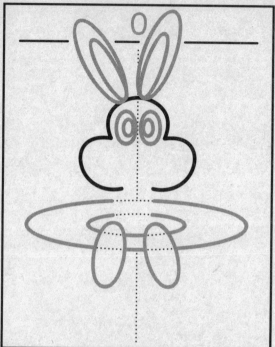

DRAW WITH NUMBERS

DRAW WITH NUMBERS

5	0
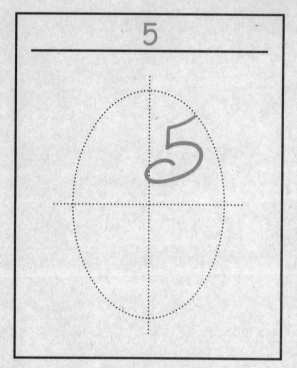	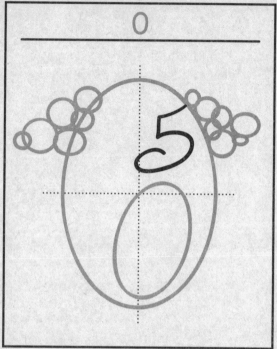
3	Finish!
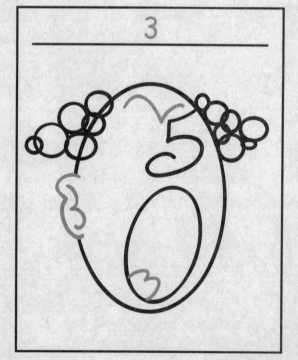	

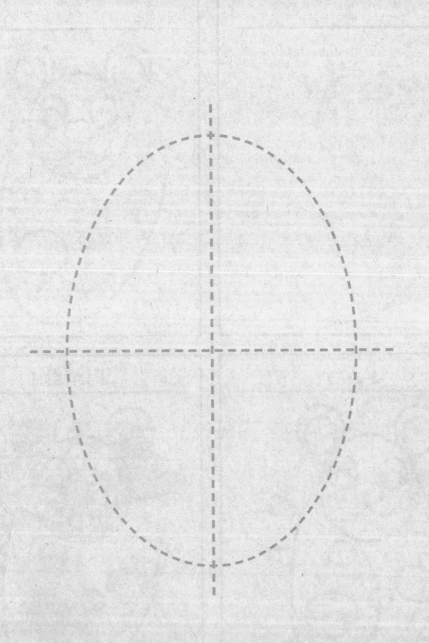

DRAW WITH NUMBERS

DRAW WITH NUMBERS

0

6

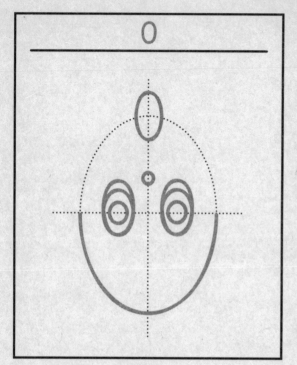

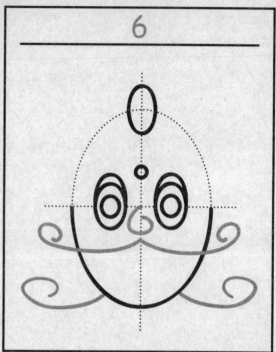

1 3

Finish!

DRAW WITH NUMBERS

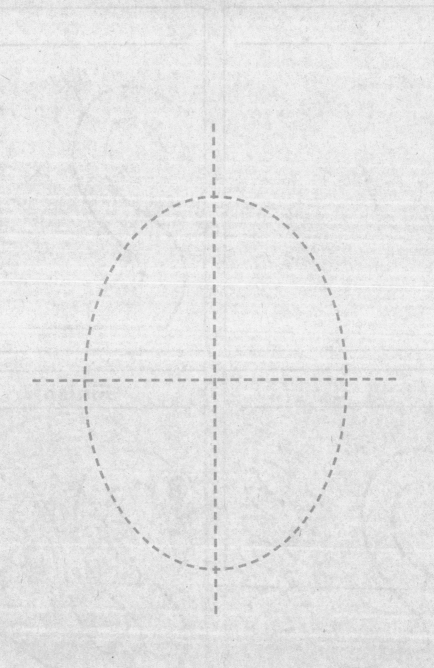

2

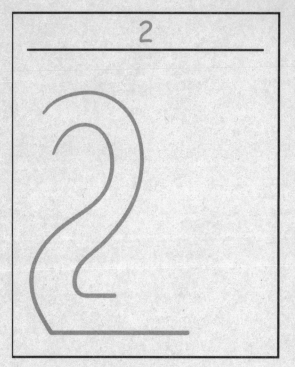

7 3

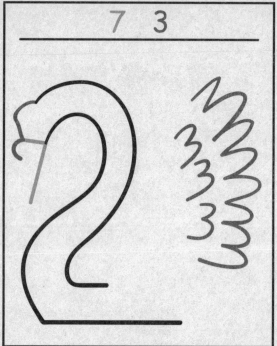

0 1

Finish!

DRAW WITH NUMBERS

DRAW WITH NUMBERS

6

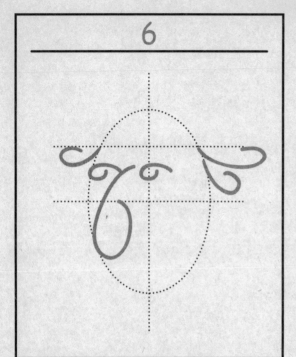

3

0

Finish!

DRAW WITH NUMBERS

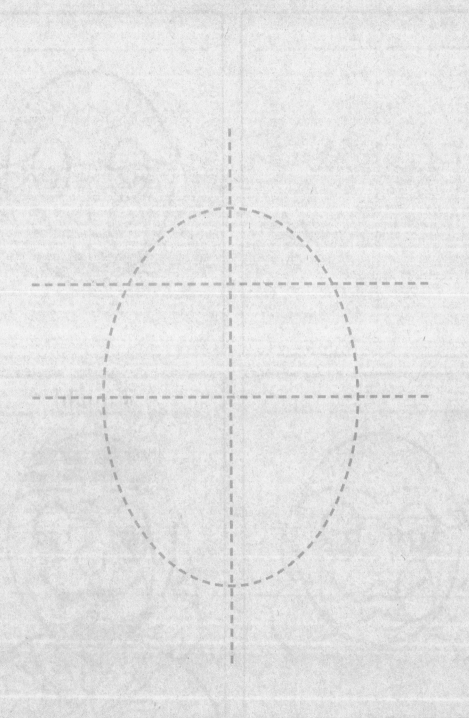

DRAW WITH NUMBERS

0 1

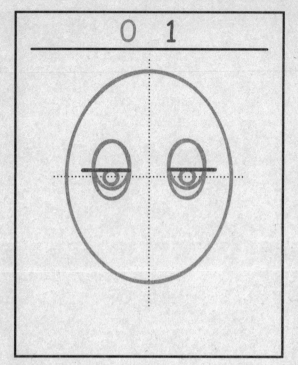

3

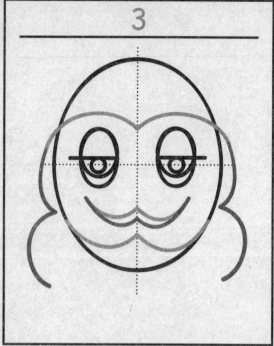

6

Finish!

DRAW WITH NUMBERS

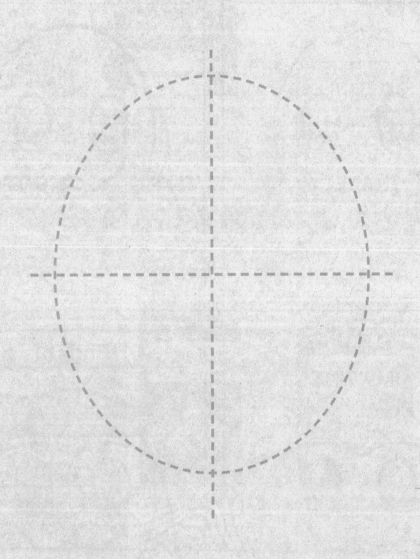

COLLECT ALL THE BOOKS
IN THE GO FUN! SERIES

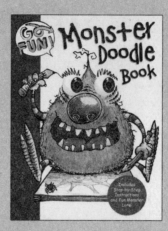

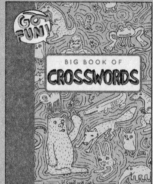